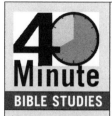

Minute

BIBLE STUDIES

6-WEEK
STUDY PROGRAM

FORGIVENESS:

BREAKING

THE POWER

OF THE PAST

PRECEPT
MINISTRIES
INTERNATIONAL

KAY ARTHUR
DAVID & BJ LAWSON

FORGIVENESS: BREAKING THE POWER OF THE PAST
PUBLISHED BY WATERBROOK PRESS
12265 Oracle Boulevard, Suite 200
Colorado Springs, Colorado 80921
A division of Random House Inc.

All Scripture quotations, are taken from the New American Standard Bible®. © Copyright
The Lockman Foundation 1960, 1962, 1963, 1968, 1971, 1972, 1973, 1975, 1977, 1995.
Used by permission. (www.Lockman.org).

ISBN 978-1-4000-7416-7

Printed in the United States of America
2007—First Edition

10 9 8 7 6 5 4 3 2 1

HOW TO USE THIS STUDY

This small-group study is for people who are interested in learning for themselves more about what the Bible says on various subjects, but who have only limited time to meet together. It's ideal, for example, for a lunch group at work, an early morning men's group, a young mothers' group meeting in a home, a Sunday-school class, or even family devotions. (It's also ideal for small groups that typically have longer meeting times—such as evening groups or Saturday morning groups—but want to devote only a portion of their time together to actual study, while reserving the rest for prayer, fellowship, or other activities.)

This book is designed so that all the group's participants will complete each lesson's study activities *at the same time.* Discussing your insights drawn from what God says about the subject reveals exciting, life-impacting truths.

Although it's a group study, you'll need a facilitator to lead the study and keep the discussion moving. (This person's function is *not* that of a lecturer or teacher. However, when this book is used in a Sunday-school class or similar setting, the teacher should feel free to lead more directly and to bring in other insights in addition to those provided in each week's lesson.)

If *you* are your group's facilitator, the leader, here are some helpful points for making your job easier:

- Go through the lesson and mark the text before you lead the group. This will give you increased familiarity with the material and will enable you to facilitate the group with greater ease. It may be easier for you to lead the group through the instructions for marking if you, as a leader, choose a specific color for each symbol you mark.

- As you lead the group, start at the beginning of the text and simply read it aloud in the order it appears in the lesson, including the "insight boxes," which appear throughout. Work through the lesson together, observing and discussing what you learn. As you read the Scripture verses, have the group say aloud the word they are marking in the text.

- The discussion questions are there simply to help you cover the material. As the class moves into the discussion, many times you will find that they will cover the questions on their own. Remember, the discussion questions are there to guide the group through the topic, not to squelch discussion.

- Remember how important it is for people to verbalize their answers and discoveries. This greatly strengthens their personal understanding of each week's lesson. Try to ensure that everyone has plenty of opportunity to contribute to each week's discussions.

- Keep the discussion moving. This may mean spending more time on some parts of the study than on others. If necessary, you should feel free to spread out a lesson over more than one session. However, remember that you don't want to slow the pace too much. It's much better to leave everyone "wanting more" than to have people dropping out because of declining interest.

- If the validity or accuracy of some of the answers seems questionable, you can gently and cheerfully remind the group to stay focused on the truth of the Scriptures. Your object is to learn what the Bible says, not to engage in human philosophy. Simply stick with the Scriptures and give God the opportunity to speak. His Word *is* truth (John 17:17)!

FORGIVENESS: BREAKING THE POWER OF THE PAST

Outside, winter pierced the day with a frigid, blustery chill; inside, a similar iciness permeated the church. Among the people gathered for the funeral, twenty family members sat scattered in eighteen pews. Snippets of conversations drifted back as I waited for the service to begin.

"Poor old soul lived alone. It was such a shame that John didn't visit his mother more than a couple of times a year."

"Did Aunt Marilyn talk to you?" "No, and I'm not talking to her until she talks to me!"

"Why didn't Rita come to the funeral?" "She got mad at Mother's funeral and hasn't talked to any of the family since."

What happened to create such division within this

family that even at a loved one's funeral they sat apart from one another and talked among themselves about other family members who weren't there?

Sadly, dysfunctional families are nothing new and hardly unusual. Dating back to the days of Cain and Abel, lack of forgiveness has destroyed countless relationships. And although our deepest hurts may come from family, forgiveness isn't simply a *family* issue; forgiveness is a *people* issue. In every relationship it's certain we'll need to extend or seek forgiveness at some point.

So this subject of forgiveness touches us all and brings to mind many questions, including…

How can I forgive when the pain is so great?

What about revenge? Is the other person going to get away with what they did?

What if I choose not to forgive?

Can I be forgiven of my past mistakes?

Does forgiving mean I have to forget the past?

For the next six weeks we'll look to the Bible for the answers to these questions and others. You'll learn how forgiveness not only cleanses your soul and frees your mind but also unlocks the chains that hold you captive to the person who wronged you.

Through this study you'll learn how to unleash the power of forgiveness in your life, letting it propel you out of painful and awkward situations and freeing you from the pain of the past.

Have you suffered pain at the hands of another person? Have you wondered if you could ever get past it?

This week we're going to look at the life of Joseph, a young man from a blended family who was horribly mistreated yet somehow broke the power of his painful past in order to walk in freedom. Let's see what we can learn from this story of pain, disappointment, and forgiveness.

OBSERVE

Leader: *Read Genesis 37:1–4. Have the group say aloud and...*

- *underline every reference to **Joseph**, including pronouns.*
- *circle every reference to **his brothers**, including synonyms and pronouns.*

As you read the text, it's helpful to have the group say the key words aloud as they mark them. This way everyone will be sure to mark every occurrence of the word, including any synonymous words or phrases. Do this throughout the study.

DISCUSS

- What did you learn from marking *Joseph*?

GENESIS 37:1–4

¹ Now Jacob lived in the land where his father had sojourned, in the land of Canaan.

² These are the records of the generations of Jacob. Joseph, when seventeen years of age, was pasturing the flock with his brothers while he was still a youth, along with the sons of Bilhah and the sons of Zilpah, his father's wives. And Joseph brought back a bad report about them to their father.

³ Now Israel [Jacob] loved Joseph more than all his sons, because he was the son of his old age; and he made him a varicolored tunic.

⁴ His brothers saw that their father loved him more than all his brothers; and so they hated him and could not speak to him on friendly terms.

• What did you learn about Joseph's relationship with his brothers? his father?

GENESIS 37:5–11

⁵ Then Joseph had a dream, and when he told it to his brothers, they hated him even more.

⁶ He said to them, "Please listen to this dream which I have had;

OBSERVE

Leader: *Read aloud Genesis 37:5–11 and have the group...*
- *circle every reference to **the brothers,** including pronouns.*
- *draw a cloud like this* ⌣⌣ *around every occurrence of the word **dream,** including pronouns.*

DISCUSS

• What did Joseph's dreams point to? Did they describe the present or the future?

• How did Joseph's brothers respond to his dreams? Did they understand them? Explain your answer.

7 for behold, we were binding sheaves in the field, and lo, my sheaf rose up and also stood erect; and behold, your sheaves gathered around and bowed down to my sheaf."

8 Then his brothers said to him, "Are you actually going to reign over us? Or are you really going to rule over us?" So they hated him even more for his dreams and for his words.

9 Now he had still another dream, and related it to his brothers, and said, "Lo, I have had still another dream; and behold, the sun and the moon and eleven stars were bowing down to me."

10 He related it to his father and to his brothers; and his father rebuked him and said to him, "What is this dream that you have had? Shall I and your mother and your brothers actually come to bow ourselves down before you to the ground?"

11 His brothers were jealous of him, but his father kept the saying in mind.

• How did his father respond to Joseph's second dream?

• Compare the responses of his brothers and father in verse 11.

GENESIS 37:18–28

18 When they [his brothers] saw him from a distance and before he came close to them, they plotted against him to put him to death.

19 They said to one another, "Here comes this dreamer!

OBSERVE

Jacob sent Joseph to check on the welfare of his brothers and the flocks in Shechem. Even though he knew they hated and envied him, Joseph obeyed his father's commands.

Leader: Read Genesis 37:18–28 aloud and have the group...

• *circle every reference to* **the brothers,** *including pronouns and synonyms such as* **one another.**

• *underline every reference to* **Joseph,** *including pronouns.*

DISCUSS

• What does this passage reveal about the relationships between various brothers and Joseph?

20 "Now then, come and let us kill him and throw him into one of the pits; and we will say, 'A wild beast devoured him.' Then let us see what will become of his dreams!"

21 But Reuben heard this and rescued him out of their hands and said, "Let us not take his life."

22 Reuben further said to them, "Shed no blood. Throw him into this pit that is in the wilderness, but do not lay hands on him"—that he might rescue him out of their hands, to restore him to his father.

23 So it came about, when Joseph reached his brothers, that they

stripped Joseph of his tunic, the varicolored tunic that was on him;

24 and they took him and threw him into the pit. Now the pit was empty, without any water in it.

25 Then they sat down to eat a meal. And as they raised their eyes and looked, behold, a caravan of Ishmaelites was coming from Gilead, with their camels bearing aromatic gum and balm and myrrh, on their way to bring them down to Egypt.

26 Judah said to his brothers, "What profit is it for us to kill our brother and cover up his blood?

• How great had the brothers' jealousy and hatred become, according to verse 18?

• As you read about the rejection and abuse Joseph suffered at the hands of his brothers, does this remind you of any similar situations of abuse, hatred, or jealousy? Do you know individuals who have been abused by their families? Discuss how it made them feel.

27 "Come and let us sell him to the Ishmaelites and not lay our hands on him, for he is our brother, our own flesh." And his brothers listened to him.

28 Then some Midianite traders passed by, so they pulled him up and lifted Joseph out of the pit, and sold him to the Ishmaelites for twenty shekels of silver. Thus they brought Joseph into Egypt.

OBSERVE

Leader: Read Genesis 37:29–36. Have the group say aloud and...
- *underline every reference to **Joseph**, including pronouns.*
- *circle every reference to **his brothers**, including pronouns.*

GENESIS 37:29–36

29 Now Reuben returned to the pit, and behold, Joseph was not in the pit; so he tore his garments.

30 He returned to his brothers and said, "The boy is not there; as for me, where am I to go?"

31 So they took Joseph's tunic, and slaughtered a male goat and dipped the tunic in the blood;

32 and they sent the varicolored tunic and brought it to their father and said, "We found this; please examine it to see whether it is your son's tunic or not."

33 Then he examined it and said, "It is my son's tunic. A wild beast has devoured him; Joseph has surely been torn to pieces!"

34 So Jacob tore his clothes, and put sack-cloth on his loins and

DISCUSS

• What did you learn about Reuben and the other brothers from this passage? What were they like? What were they doing?

• How was their father affected by their choices?

• What happened to Joseph?

• Parents often are hurt by their children's actions. Do you know parents who have been wounded by something their child did? Discuss the scenario.

mourned for his son many days.

35 Then all his sons and all his daughters arose to comfort him, but he refused to be comforted. And he said, "Surely I will go down to Sheol [the grave] in mourning for my son." So his father wept for him.

36 Meanwhile, the Midianites sold him in Egypt to Potiphar, Pharaoh's officer, the captain of the bodyguard.

GENESIS 42:1–17

¹ Now Jacob saw that there was grain in Egypt, and Jacob said to his sons, "Why are you staring at one another?"

² He said, "Behold, I have heard that there is grain in Egypt; go down there and buy some for us from that place, so that we may live and not die."

³ Then ten brothers of Joseph went down to buy grain from Egypt.

⁴ But Jacob did not send Joseph's brother Benjamin with his brothers, for he said, "I am afraid that harm may befall him."

⁵ So the sons of Israel came to buy grain among those

OBSERVE

Some years after the brothers sold Joseph into slavery, he accurately interpreted Pharaoh's dream to predict that Egypt would have seven years of plenty followed by seven years of famine. Pharaoh promoted the one-time slave to be his second in command of all Egypt. During the plentiful years Joseph stored grain in great abundance. When the seven years of famine came, he opened the storehouse and sold grain to people from all over the face of the earth. This chain of events led to Joseph's next encounter with his brothers, twenty-two years after they betrayed him.

Leader: Read Genesis 42:1–17 aloud and have the group...
- *underline every reference to **Joseph,** including pronouns.*
- *circle every reference to **his brothers,** including pronouns and synonyms such as **sons of Israel.***

DISCUSS

• What did you learn from marking the references to Joseph's brothers?

• What did they claim to be in verse 11? Are they?

who were coming, for the famine was in the land of Canaan also.

6 Now Joseph was the ruler over the land; he was the one who sold to all the people of the land. And Joseph's brothers came and bowed down to him with their faces to the ground.

7 When Joseph saw his brothers he recognized them, but he disguised himself to them and spoke to them harshly. And he said to them, "Where have you come from?" And they said, "From the land of Canaan, to buy food."

8 But Joseph had recognized his brothers, although they did not recognize him.

⁹ Joseph remembered the dreams which he had about them, and said to them, "You are spies; you have come to look at the undefended parts of our land."

¹⁰ Then they said to him, "No, my lord, but your servants have come to buy food.

¹¹ "We are all sons of one man; we are honest men, your servants are not spies."

¹² Yet he said to them, "No, but you have come to look at the undefended parts of our land!"

¹³ But they said, "Your servants are twelve brothers in all, the sons of one man in

• What is so significant about this passage? What did the brothers do when they appeared before Joseph?

• What does this tell you about God? about Joseph's dreams? Is this all coincidence, or is God at work? Discuss.

• How did Joseph treat his brothers? Why did he deal with them in this manner, and what was the result?

the land of Canaan; and behold, the youngest is with our father today, and one is no longer alive."

14 Joseph said to them, "It is as I said to you, you are spies;

15 by this you will be tested: by the life of Pharaoh, you shall not go from this place unless your youngest brother comes here!

16 "Send one of you that he may get your brother, while you remain confined, that your words may be tested, whether there is truth in you. But if not, by the life of Pharaoh, surely you are spies."

17 So he put them all together in prison for three days.

GENESIS 42:21–24

21 Then they [the brothers] said to one another, "Truly we are guilty concerning our brother [Joseph], because we saw the distress of his soul when he pleaded with us, yet we would not listen; therefore this distress has come upon us."

22 Reuben answered them, saying, "Did I not tell you, 'Do not sin against the boy'; and you would not listen? Now comes the reckoning for his blood."

23 They did not know, however, that Joseph understood, for there was an interpreter between them.

OBSERVE

Leader: Read Genesis 42:21–24 aloud and have the group…

- *underline every reference to **Joseph**, including pronouns.*
- *circle every reference to **his brothers**, including pronouns.*
- *mark the word **sin** with a slash, like this:* ⁄

DISCUSS

- What new insight did you gain about how Joseph responded when his brothers threw him into the pit?

- Have you ever pleaded with someone to stop doing something wrong or hurtful? What happened?

- What did you learn from marking the references to the brothers in this passage?

• How did Joseph respond when he heard his brothers talking after they arrived in Egypt? What does this reveal about him?

• What does this passage tell you about the guilt of sin?

OBSERVE

As the brothers left Egypt, leaving Simeon behind, Joseph had the money they'd paid hidden in their sacks of grain. This served as a test designed to break their hard hearts. The famine continued, and they returned to Egypt with Benjamin as Joseph had requested. Simeon was returned to them, they received more grain, and the brothers headed home. Benjamin was soon arrested for stealing a silver cup, hidden in his sack at Joseph's command, and they all had to return to the palace. This was yet another test to bring them to a point of brokenness. Judah interceded for the boy and offered himself in Benjamin's place, revealing a change in his heart and an indication of the brothers' repentance concerning Joseph.

24 He turned away from them and wept. But when he returned to them and spoke to them, he took Simeon from them and bound him before their eyes.

GENESIS 45:1–15

1 Then Joseph could not control himself before all those who stood by him, and he cried, "Have everyone go out from me." So there was no man with him when Joseph made himself known to his brothers.

2 He wept so loudly that the Egyptians heard it, and the household of Pharaoh heard of it.

3 Then Joseph said to his brothers, "I am

Joseph! Is my father still alive?" But his brothers could not answer him, for they were dismayed at his presence.

4 Then Joseph said to his brothers, "Please come closer to me." And they came closer. And he said, "I am your brother Joseph, whom you sold into Egypt.

5 "Now do not be grieved or angry with yourselves, because you sold me here, for God sent me before you to preserve life.

6 "For the famine has been in the land these two years, and there are still five years in which there will be neither plowing nor harvesting.

Leader: Read Genesis 45:1–15 aloud. Have the group…
  • *underline every reference to **Joseph**, including pronouns.*
  • *circle every reference to **his brothers**, including pronouns.*

DISCUSS

• Briefly summarize the events in this passage.

• What did you learn from marking *Joseph*?

• Did Joseph ignore or deny his brothers' wrongdoing?

• How did Joseph deal with his brothers?

• What does this tell you about Joseph? about his belief in and relationship to God?

7 "God sent me before you to preserve for you a remnant in the earth, and to keep you alive by a great deliverance.

8 "Now, therefore, it was not you who sent me here, but God; and He has made me a father to Pharaoh and lord of all his household and ruler over all the land of Egypt.

9 "Hurry and go up to my father, and say to him, 'Thus says your son Joseph, "God has made me lord of all Egypt; come down to me, do not delay.

10 "You shall live in the land of Goshen, and you shall be near me, you and your children and your children's

children and your flocks and your herds and all that you have.

11 "There I will also provide for you, for there are still five years of famine to come, and you and your household and all that you have would be impoverished." '

12 "Behold, your eyes see, and the eyes of my brother Benjamin see, that it is my mouth which is speaking to you.

13 "Now you must tell my father of all my splendor in Egypt, and all that you have seen; and you must hurry and bring my father down here."

• Did Joseph wait for his brothers to ask for forgiveness before he gave it? What lessons do you find here for our own behavior? Discuss your answer.

• Instead of harboring bitterness or returning hatred for hatred, Joseph looked beyond his brothers to see the hand of God. We often interpret our tragedies as injustices or punishments for unknown faults. But we need to understand that God sometimes leads His children into suffering so that He might bring out of that suffering some greater good. Can you think of a time when you've seen God work this way?

Leader: If time allows, invite someone in the group to share a personal experience of seeing God bring good out of suffering.

14 Then he fell on his brother Benjamin's neck and wept, and Benjamin wept on his neck. 15 He kissed all his brothers and wept on them, and afterward his brothers talked with him.

OBSERVE

The family accepted Joseph's invitation and moved to Egypt to live under his generous care. But Jacob's death several years later prompted fresh concern among Joseph's brothers. Let's look at their conversation.

Leader: Read aloud Genesis 50:15–21. Have the group...
- *underline every reference to **Joseph**, including pronouns.*
- *mark each occurrence of the word **forgive** with a big **X**.*

GENESIS 50:15–21

15 When Joseph's brothers saw that their father was dead, they said, "What if Joseph bears a grudge against us and pays us back in full for all the wrong which we did to him!" 16 So they sent a message to Joseph, saying, "Your father charged before he died, saying,

17 'Thus you shall say to Joseph, "Please forgive, I beg you, the transgression of your brothers and their sin, for they did you wrong." ' And now, please forgive the transgression of the servants of the God of your father." And Joseph wept when they spoke to him.

18 Then his brothers also came and fell down before him and said, "Behold, we are your servants."

19 But Joseph said to them, "Do not be afraid, for am I in God's place?

20 "As for you, you meant evil against me, but God meant it for

DISCUSS

• Now that their father was dead, what was the brothers' concern? Did it seem to be warranted? Explain your answer.

• Is this the first record of the brothers' confession of their sin?

• What is confirmed about Joseph in this passage?

• Do you see any possible connection between verses 15 and 19? Who can rightfully judge and punish sin?

• What shows that Joseph truly forgave his brothers?

• Romans 15:4 tells us that the Old Testament was written for our instruction and to give us encouragement and hope. What did you learn from Joseph's life that can help you?

good in order to bring about this present result, to preserve many people alive.

21 "So therefore, do not be afraid; I will provide for you and your little ones." So he comforted them and spoke kindly to them.

WRAP IT UP

As believers we can refuse to allow the past to determine our future. Everything you have endured, suffered, and experienced can have eternal value if you choose to view it from God's perspective.

Joseph's life clearly demonstrates this principle. He suffered a terrible crime at the hand of his brothers, who initially schemed to kill him before selling him into slavery. Yet Joseph did not hold it against them. Instead, years later when famine drove the brothers to Egypt in search of food, Joseph recognized them and felt compassion for them before they knew who he was. He forgave them unconditionally—not dependent on any show of remorse from them. In fact, although they were humble before Joseph, they never specifically asked forgiveness from him. To be sure, they had mistreated him, but he chose to see the past from God's point of view. He recognized that God was working His good in Joseph's life through the very evil that had been done to him.

Joseph's example reminds us that when we don't know why certain things happen, we must remain confident that God is at work in every experience of our lives, even the painful ones. Instead of allowing his situation to paralyze him or render him ineffective, Joseph believed God had a plan for his life. By fulfilling that plan and looking ahead, he broke the power of the past—a past riddled with wounds inflicted by others.

What about you? Do you believe God has a plan and purpose for your life? Are you willing to do what it takes to break the power of the past and walk in freedom toward the future?

Last week we saw the wounds Joseph suffered at the hands of his brothers and how he chose to forgive them. Have you forgiven those who have wounded you? Or does your stomach knot up when a particular person crosses your path? Do you perhaps even avoid certain events or places if you believe that person will be there?

It has been said that clinging to resentment is like taking poison and waiting for the other person to die. This week we'll look at why forgiveness is necessary and at the impact forgiving someone—or refusing to forgive—can have on your life.

OBSERVE

The Sermon on the Mount lays the foundation for Jesus' instructions to His disciples, setting forth the basics of the believer's walk. This instruction included His teaching on prayer—a pattern for prayer actually. Let's see what we can learn from this pattern, often called the Lord's Prayer.

Leader: Read Matthew 6:9–13 aloud and have the group...
- *mark the words **forgive** and **forgiven** with a big **X**.*
- *draw a box around the words **debts** and **debtors.***

MATTHEW 6:9–13

9 "Pray, then, in this way: 'Our Father who is in heaven, hallowed be Your name.

10 'Your kingdom come. Your will be done, on earth as it is in heaven.

11 'Give us this day our daily bread.

12 'And forgive us our debts, as we also have forgiven our debtors.

13 'And do not lead us into temptation, but deliver us from evil. [For Yours is the kingdom and the power and the glory forever. Amen.]' "

DISCUSS

• Discuss what you learned from marking *forgive* and *forgiven*.

• What do you think "as we" implies in verse 12? Explain your answer.

• What did Jesus indicate we're to ask forgiveness for?

• How would you define *debts*?

LUKE 11:2–4

2 And He said to them, "When you pray, say: 'Father, hallowed be Your name. Your kingdom come.

3 'Give us each day our daily bread.

OBSERVE

Is Jesus referring to a financial obligation when He speaks of "debts"? In order to answer this question, let's look at Luke 11:2–4, a parallel passage with some clear similarities to Matthew 6.

Leader: Read aloud Luke 11:2–4.

  • *Have the group say aloud and mark each occurrence of **forgive** with an X.*

DISCUSS

• From what you saw in this passage, was Jesus referring to debt as a financial obligation? If not, what did He mean by debt?

OBSERVE

Let's return to Matthew 6, where immediately after closing His model prayer with "amen," Jesus added a few words about forgiveness.

Leader: Read Matthew 6:14–15 and have the group...

• *mark each occurrence of **forgive** with an X.*

• *draw a jagged line over the word **but**, like this:* ⋀⋁⋁

DISCUSS

• You may be asking, "Why should I forgive? It's so painful." What important insight did Jesus give in verses 14 and 15 about the *why* of forgiveness?

4 'And forgive us our sins, for we ourselves also forgive everyone who is indebted to us. And lead us not into temptation.' "

MATTHEW 6:14–15

14 "For if you forgive others for their transgressions, your heavenly Father will also forgive you.

15 "But if you do not forgive others, then your Father will not forgive your transgressions."

• What did you learn from marking *forgive* in these verses?

• Discuss how what you've observed relates to verse 14.

MATTHEW 18:21–27

21 Then Peter came and said to Him, "Lord, how often shall my brother sin against me and I forgive him? Up to seven times?"

22 Jesus said to him, "I do not say to you, up to seven times, but up to seventy times seven.

23 "For this reason the kingdom of heaven may be compared to a king who wished to settle accounts with his slaves.

OBSERVE

Jesus gave a great illustration of forgiveness in the following parable.

Leader: Read Matthew 18:21–27. Have the group say aloud and...
- *mark each occurrence of **forgive** and related words with an **X**, as before.*
- *mark every reference to **the king**, including pronouns and synonyms like **lord**, with a **K**.*
- *draw a box around the words **owed** and **debt**.*

DISCUSS

• According to verses 21–22, what prompted Jesus to tell this story?

INSIGHT

It's important to understand the context of this parable. According to the common rabbinic thought of the day, offended persons only had to forgive three times, so Peter thought he was being generous by suggesting "up to seven times." Jesus' answer probably stunned the disciples. Essentially, He was saying that love doesn't keep score, just as 1 Corinthians 13:5 declares. The right thing to do is to forgive from the heart.

• Discuss what you learned from marking the references to *the king*.

• What did the slave promise to do? How did the king respond?

• As a slave, was it likely he could pay the debt?

• What did you learn from marking *forgive* and related words?

24 "When he had begun to settle them, one who owed him ten thousand talents was brought to him.

25 "But since he did not have the means to repay, his lord commanded him to be sold, along with his wife and children and all that he had, and repayment to be made.

26 "So the slave fell to the ground and prostrated himself before him, saying, 'Have patience with me and I will repay you everything.'

27 "And the lord of that slave felt compassion and released him and forgave him the debt."

• Whom do you think the king represents in this parable? Explain your answer.

• Whom do you think the servant represents? Explain your answer.

MATTHEW 18:28–35

28 "But that slave went out and found one of his fellow slaves who owed him a hundred denarii; and he seized him and began to choke him, saying, 'Pay back what you owe.'

29 "So his fellow slave fell to the ground and began to plead with him, saying, 'Have patience with me and I will repay you.'

OBSERVE

Now let's see how the slave behaves in light of his canceled debt.

Leader: Read aloud Matthew 18:28–35 and have the group...
- *draw a box around the words **owe, owed,** and **debt.***
- *mark each occurrence of **forgive** and related words with an **X.***

DISCUSS

• Discuss what you learned from these verses about the slave who had been forgiven.

• Compare verses 26 and 29. What do you notice?

INSIGHT

The denarius was a coin with a value approximately equal to the average day's wage for a common laborer in Jesus' day. By contrast, the talent was the largest monetary unit. A man might work as long as twenty years to earn that much, so ten thousand talents would have been a nearly inconceivable debt.[1]

• According to verse 32, why did the king forgive the wicked slave in the first place?

• According to verse 33, how did the king expect the wicked slave to treat his fellow slave and why?

• What comparison can you draw between the king's expectation of the slave, as described in verse 33, and God's expectation of us, as seen in Matthew 6:14–15?

1 Warren Weirsbe: "Matthew" in *The Bible Exposition Commentary: An Exposition of the New Testament Comprising the Entire "Be" Series,* Vol. 1 (Colorado Springs, CO: ChariotVictor Publishing, 1989), 67.

30 "But he was unwilling and went and threw him in prison until he should pay back what was owed.

31 "So when his fellow slaves saw what had happened, they were deeply grieved and came and reported to their lord all that had happened.

32 "Then summoning him, his lord said to him, 'You wicked slave, I forgave you all that debt because you pleaded with me.

33 'Should you not also have had mercy on your fellow slave, in the same way that I had mercy on you?'

34 "And his lord, moved with anger, handed him over to the torturers until he should repay all that was owed him.

35 "My heavenly Father will also do the same to you, if each of you does not forgive his brother from your heart."

• According to verse 34, what happened to the wicked slave because he refused to forgive?

INSIGHT

Torturers, a noun derived from the Greek verb *basanizō,* is used elsewhere to refer to sicknesses (Matthew 4:24; 8:6) and adverse circumstances (Matthew 14:24). God uses these things to correct wrong attitudes and produce proper spirits in His children (1 Corinthians 11:30–32). These torturers may be seen in our lives as difficult circumstances, sickness, bitterness, jealousy, anger, etc. Remember, Jesus is addressing Peter and the other disciples; His message is directed to believers, not unbelievers.

• According to what you've seen in Matthew 18 and the Insight Box, how does Jesus' teaching apply to our lives today? Is refusing to forgive a valid choice for a believer?

OBSERVE

Next let's look at some instructions from the apostle Paul to us as believers. Having admonished us to behave differently than we did before receiving Christ, he then gave an example of how this change should look.

Leader: *Read Ephesians 4:30–32 and Colossians 3:13.*

- *Have the group mark **forgiving** with an* **X.**

DISCUSS

- Based on what you read in this passage, what grieves the Holy Spirit?

- What did you learn about forgiveness from these verses and how should it affect our relationships?

- Before you proceed with this lesson, stop and ask yourself if there's anyone you need to forgive. When you think of hurt or disappointment, does someone specific come to mind? Are there people you refuse to love or do good to when you

EPHESIANS 4:30–32

30 Do not grieve the Holy Spirit of God, by whom you were sealed for the day of redemption.

31 Let all bitterness and wrath and anger and clamor and slander be put away from you, along with all malice.

32 Be kind to one another, tender-hearted, forgiving each other, just as God in Christ also has forgiven you.

COLOSSIANS 3:13

13 Bearing with one another, and forgiving each other, whoever has a complaint against anyone; just as the Lord forgave you, so also should you.

have the opportunity? Does your stomach knot up when a certain person comes your way? Is there an individual whom you avoid at all costs?

Leader: *Give the group time to reflect on these questions.*

• If a name comes to mind when contemplating these questions, don't ignore it. Write it down—along with the offense.

OBSERVE

As we bring this week to a close, let's take a look at two more verses God has given us to reinforce an important principle.

INSIGHT

Mercy in the following passages carries the idea of showing mercy, extending help, forgiving, and being generous. It implies not only a compassion related to the misfortune of others but also an active desire to remove the cause.

Leader: *Read aloud Matthew 5:7 and James 2:13.*

   • *Have the group draw a squiggly line under the words* **merciful, mercy,** *and* **merciless,** *like this:* ◡◡◡◡◠

DISCUSS

• What did you learn from marking the references to mercy?

• How do these verses relate to what we learned from Jesus' teaching on forgiveness?

• How do these verses compare with Matthew 18:33, in which the king said to the servant whom he had forgiven a great debt, "Should you not also have had mercy on your fellow slave, in the same way that I had mercy on you?"

MATTHEW 5:7

7 "Blessed are the merciful, for they shall receive mercy."

JAMES 2:13

13 For judgment will be merciless to one who has shown no mercy; mercy triumphs over judgment.

WRAP IT UP

Doctors have long suspected—and with today's modern technology have confirmed—that people who don't forgive tend to be sick. Often physical illness directly results from an unforgiving spirit. Our bodies are not designed to bear the burden of bitterness and anger; in the long run, they break down one way or another under the stress and strain. This doesn't mean that everyone who is sick needs to forgive someone; it does, however, mean that long-term refusal to forgive can cause physical afflictions.

Are you suffering from stomach trouble, heart palpitations, or inability to sleep? Is it possible these symptoms ultimately come from an unforgiving heart rather than strictly from physical causes? Could they be the torturers? Ask the Lord to give you some answers.

If we refuse to let go of the pain of injustice, or if we strive to get even, we put ourselves in an emotional prison—the worst kind of captivity. But when we extend mercy and forgiveness, sharing with others what God has shared with us, we enjoy glorious freedom.

Forgive! This is what Jesus taught Peter and the other disciples: you've been forgiven, so now live as a person of forgiveness. Give up your claim to be right, which really doesn't matter. Instead, trust God to deal with your offenders. If you will listen to the Spirit's leading and choose to walk His way of forgiveness, you will be healthier in soul and body. Your relationships with God and man will be drastically changed. Your prayer life will improve. The captive will be set free!

To truly understand your responsibility to forgive others, you must first realize that no matter what you have done, God assures you of complete and absolute forgiveness through the death of His Son. As we've seen, Jesus said we are to forgive *as* we have been forgiven. If you do not believe you've been fully forgiven of all *your* sins, it will be impossible to forgive those who have sinned against you.

This week we want to look at the forgiveness God extends to us and how that affects our responsibility toward others.

OBSERVE

The book of Romans is a letter written by the apostle Paul to believers in Rome to explain key truths of the gospel, the "good news" of Jesus Christ. In the verses we're going to look at, when he used the pronoun *we,* he was including himself, his companions, and all those who were formerly ungodly sinners, enemies of God. Just prior to this passage, Paul was speaking of Jews who rely upon the Law of Moses.

Leader: Read Romans 3:9–12 and 23 aloud. Have the group...

* *mark the words* **sin** *and* **sinned** *with a slash, like this:* /
* *mark the word* **righteous** *with an* **R.**

ROMANS 3:9–12, 23

9 What then? Are we better than they? Not at all; for we have already charged that both Jews and Greeks are all under sin;

10 as it is written, "There is none righteous, not even one;

11 There is none who understands, there is none who seeks for God;

¹² All have turned aside, together they have become useless; there is none who does good, there is not even one."

²³ For all have sinned and fall short of the glory of God.

INSIGHT

The Greek word used here for *sin* literally means "to miss the mark, to fall short of a standard, to do or go wrong, to violate God's law."

Righteous means "to be free of guilt and sin; to be conformed to God's standard, not man's."

DISCUSS

• What did you learn from marking *sin* and *sinned* in these verses?

• According to the Word of God, how widespread is sin? Who can claim to be without sin?

OBSERVE

We just saw that all are sinners, but how did this come to be true?

Leader: *Read Romans 5:12. Have the group say aloud and…*

- *mark the words **sin** and **sinned** with a slash.*
- *draw a tombstone over each occurrence of the word **death**, like this:* ⌂

DISCUSS

- How did we become sinners?

- What was the result of sin entering into the world?

OBSERVE

But God doesn't want us to die, to be separated from Him for all eternity. Therefore what did He do?

Leader: *Read Matthew 1:18–23 and 2 Corinthians 5:21 aloud. Have the group…*

- *mark each reference to **Jesus**, including pronouns and synonyms such as **the child**, with a cross:* ✝
- *draw a slash through the words **sin** and **sins**.*

ROMANS 5:12

12 Therefore, just as through one man [Adam] sin entered into the world, and death through sin, and so death spread to all men, because all sinned.

MATTHEW 1:18–23

18 Now the birth of Jesus Christ was as follows: when His mother Mary had been betrothed to Joseph, before they came together she was found to be with child by the Holy Spirit.

19 And Joseph her husband, being a righteous man and not

wanting to disgrace her, planned to send her away secretly.

20 But when he had considered this, behold, an angel of the Lord appeared to him in a dream, saying, "Joseph, son of David, do not be afraid to take Mary as your wife; for the Child who has been conceived in her is of the Holy Spirit.

21 "She will bear a Son; and you shall call His name Jesus, for He will save His people from their sins."

22 Now all this took place to fulfill what was spoken by the Lord through the prophet:

DISCUSS

• According to Matthew 1:18–23, was Jesus born a sinner? Explain your answer.

• What did Jesus do for us, according to 2 Corinthians 5:21, and what was the result?

• If Jesus wasn't a sinner, did He have to die? Why did He die?

23 "Behold, the virgin shall be with child and shall bear a Son, and they shall call His name Immanuel," which translated means, "God with us."

2 CORINTHIANS 5:21

21 He [God] made Him [Jesus] who knew no sin to be sin on our behalf, so that we might become the righteousness of God in Him.

OBSERVE

We've seen that Jesus died for our sins. Now the questions are, what was our condition before He died for us, and how has His death changed our situation?

Leader: Read Romans 5:6–10 and 6:23. Have the group say aloud and...

• *circle every reference to **believers**, including the pronouns **we, us,** and **our**.*

• *mark each reference to **Christ**, including synonyms and pronouns, with a cross.*

ROMANS 5:6–10

6 For while we were still helpless, at the right time Christ died for the ungodly.

7 For one will hardly die for a righteous man; though perhaps for the good man someone would dare even to die.

8 But God demonstrates His own love toward us, in that while we were yet sinners, Christ died for us.

9 Much more then, having now been justified by His blood, we shall be saved from the wrath of God through Him.

10 For if while we were enemies we were reconciled to God through the death of His Son, much more, having been reconciled, we shall be saved by His life.

ROMANS 6:23

23 For the wages of sin is death, but the free gift of God is eternal life in Christ Jesus our Lord.

DISCUSS

• What did you learn from marking the references to *Christ*, God's Son?

• What words were used to describe our condition in these verses?

• When did God demonstrate His love for us?

• At what point did we receive the Lord's forgiveness?

• What free gift has Jesus provided for us?

OBSERVE

Leader: Read Colossians 1:21–22 and 2 Corinthians 5:18–20 aloud. Have the group…

• *draw a box around each occurrence of the words **reconciled, reconciling, and reconciliation**.*

• *underline the phrase __not counting their trespasses against them__.*

INSIGHT

The word *reconciliation* assumes a quarrel or breach of friendship. *To reconcile* means "to change or exchange." Here the term is associated with changing a relationship from enmity to friendship.

Man's sin created a barrier between him and God. Reconciliation to God signifies complete forgiveness and the establishing of a relationship with Him.

Reconciliation is unique to the Christian faith. Every other religion teaches that man has to appease God. Biblical Christianity teaches that God appeases Himself, supplying what is necessary to reconcile us to Him: His Son's blood for forgiveness of our sins.

DISCUSS

• What did you learn from marking *reconciled* and related words?

COLOSSIANS 1:21–22

21 And although you were formerly alienated and hostile in mind, engaged in evil deeds,

22 yet He has now reconciled you in His fleshly body through death, in order to present you before Him holy and blameless and beyond reproach.

2 CORINTHIANS 5:18–20

18 Now all these things are from God, who reconciled us to Himself through Christ and gave us the ministry of reconciliation,

19 namely, that God was in Christ reconciling the world to Himself, not counting their trespasses against

them, and He has committed to us the word of reconciliation.

20 Therefore, we are ambassadors for Christ, as though God were making an appeal through us; we beg you on behalf of Christ, be reconciled to God.

• What were you like before you were reconciled to God? After?

• If we've been reconciled, what has happened to our trespasses?

• How did Jesus' forgiveness demonstrate His love for us?

• Keeping in mind all we have learned, how do we demonstrate God's love for others?

INSIGHT

An *ambassador* is an authorized messenger or person representing a higher authority. In this context the ambassador is a messenger of Christ carrying the message of reconciliation.

• What is our responsibility in reconciliation? Can you fulfill that responsibility if you refuse to forgive? Explain your answer.

OBSERVE

As you have seen, you don't have to remain a slave to sin—you can be reconciled to God. Let's take one more look at the gospel and what it means to us before we wrap up this lesson.

Leader: Read 1 Corinthians 15:1–8 aloud. Have the group...

- *mark every reference to **the gospel**, including the pronoun **which**, with a* **G.**
- *mark each reference to **Christ**, including pronouns, with a cross.* †
- *underline the phrase __according to the Scriptures__.*

DISCUSS

- What did you learn from marking all the references to the gospel?

- Just so we don't miss it, what are the main points of the gospel according to verses 3 and 4?

1 CORINTHIANS 15:1–8

¹ Now I make known to you, brethren, the gospel which I preached to you, which also you received, in which also you stand,

² by which also you are saved, if you hold fast the word which I preached to you, unless you believed in vain.

³ For I delivered to you as of first importance what I also received, that Christ died for our sins according to the Scriptures,

⁴ and that He was buried, and that He was raised on the third day according to the Scriptures,

5 and that He appeared to Cephas, then to the twelve.

6 After that He appeared to more than five hundred brethren at one time, most of whom remain until now, but some have fallen asleep;

7 then He appeared to James, then to all the apostles;

8 and last of all, as to one untimely born, He appeared to me also.

• What happened "according to the Scriptures"?

• In verses 5 through 8, what evidence did Paul cite to affirm that these things actually occurred?

• According to the gospel, who paid for your sins? How was the payment made?

• Discuss how this relates to our study of forgiveness to this point. What does understanding that *we* have been forgiven have to do with our forgiving *others?*

WRAP IT UP

Sin is an unpopular word, but it describes our violations of God's laws. We are responsible for our sins—the Bible is clear on this matter. However, Jesus already has paid for all your sins—past, present, and future (Titus 3:4–7). You can deal responsibly with sin now and receive God's forgiveness, or you can ignore it, make excuses, continue in sin, and receive God's judgment.

You may have heard someone say, "I can't forgive myself!" Perhaps you've recited this mantra yourself. Yet in all we've read so far, nowhere have we seen that we are to forgive ourselves. To buy into that thinking means we don't have a true understanding of God's forgiveness. We'd be saying God's love and provision wasn't enough. In a sense we'd be placing ourselves above God.

To refuse to believe you are forgiven is to turn your back on the love of God: "For God so loved the world, that He gave His only begotten Son, that whoever believes in Him shall not perish, but have eternal life" (John 3:16). Perhaps you need to stop at this point and ask yourself, "Have I received God's gift of forgiveness and His promise of eternal life through Jesus Christ?" If not, why wait? If this is the desire of your heart, talk to your small-group leader, who will gladly pray with you and welcome you into God's kingdom.

Have you made a mess of your life? Do you feel unworthy of the Father's love? Having seen for yourself what God says, do you realize that no matter what you have done, you can be assured of complete and absolute forgiveness? Whether you have brought shame on your family, squandered family finances, been involved in sexually immoral relationships or pornography, stolen from someone, or even murdered, it's not too late. Will you receive His forgiveness now? Here's how:

1. First, **agree with God that you have sinned—broken His holy law, rebelled against His holy will.** Name your sins for what they are. The word *confess* in 1 John 1:9 means "to say the same thing." To confess sin, then, is to agree with God that what you have done is wrong.

2. **Take responsibility for your sins.** You can't blame anyone else. Acknowledge your sins and take full responsibility.

3. **Tell God you're willing to make restitution if necessary.** This willingness to be right not just with God but also with man follows the principle Jesus laid down for us in Matthew 5:23–24.

4. **Thank God for the blood of Jesus Christ that cleanses you from all sin and in faith accept His forgiveness.** Remember, forgiveness is always based on grace, never merit. Where sin did abound, grace did much more abound (Romans 5:20).

5. **Take God at His Word.** "Therefore there is now no condemnation for those who are in Christ Jesus" (Romans 8:1). No matter your feelings, cling in faith to what God says. Don't let Satan, the accuser of the brethren, rob you of faith's victory.

6. **Thank God for the gift of His Holy Spirit, and tell Him that you want to walk by the Spirit so that you will not fulfill the lusts of the flesh** (Galatians 5:16). Prayers like this show genuine repentance.

Once you accept God's forgiveness, you have the foundation to forgive others and to walk in true freedom.

You want me to forgive?! How can I forgive someone who has hurt me so deeply? Do you know what they did to me? Perhaps this is your response to what you have learned in the study so far. This week we will see how we can forgive even the most horrible of offenses against us.

OBSERVE

Leader: *Read aloud Galatians 5:19–21, Ephesians 5:3–6, and 1 Corinthians 6:9–11.*

• *Have the group underline* **will not inherit the kingdom of God, neither…will inherit the kingdom of God,** *and* **inheritance in the kingdom of God.**

DISCUSS

• According to these passages, what characterizes those who will not inherit the kingdom of God?

GALATIANS 5:19–21

19 Now the deeds of the flesh are evident, which are: immorality, impurity, sensuality,

20 idolatry, sorcery, enmities, strife, jealousy, outbursts of anger, disputes, dissensions, factions,

21 envying, drunkenness, carousing, and things like these, of which I forewarn you, just as I have forewarned you, that those who practice such things will not inherit the kingdom of God.

EPHESIANS 5:3–6

3 But immorality or any impurity or greed must not even be named among you, as is proper among saints;

4 and there must be no filthiness and silly talk, or coarse jesting, which are not fitting, but rather giving of thanks.

5 For this you know with certainty, that no immoral or impure person or covetous man, who is an idolater, has an inheritance in the kingdom of Christ and God.

6 Let no one deceive you with empty words, for because of these things the wrath of God comes upon the sons of disobedience.

• Have you or someone you love been hurt by someone committing these sins? Have you been hurt by an alcoholic parent? Have you been sexually abused?

• According to 1 Corinthians 6:10, will these people be in the kingdom of God if they don't accept Christ?

• First Corinthians 6:11 says, "Such were some of you." Often in Scripture the word *but* shows a contrast taking place. What do you learn from this verse by noting what is being contrasted and how that relates to our study of forgiveness? Explain your answer.

• If those who've hurt us through their sin repent, God will allow them into heaven, and if they don't, God will deal with them. Our responsibility is to forgive.

1 CORINTHIANS 6:9–11

⁹ Or do you not know that the unrighteous will not inherit the kingdom of God? Do not be deceived; neither fornicators, nor idolaters, nor adulterers, nor effeminate, nor homosexuals,

¹⁰ nor thieves, nor the covetous, nor drunkards, nor revilers, nor swindlers, will inherit the kingdom of God.

¹¹ Such were some of you; but you were washed, but you were sanctified, but you were justified in the name of the Lord Jesus Christ and in the Spirit of our God.

COLOSSIANS 3:1–10

1 Therefore if you have been raised up with Christ, keep seeking the things above, where Christ is, seated at the right hand of God.

2 Set your mind on the things above, not on the things that are on earth.

3 For you have died and your life is hidden with Christ in God.

4 When Christ, who is our life, is revealed, then you also will be revealed with Him in glory.

5 Therefore consider the members of your earthly body as dead to immorality, impurity, passion, evil desire, and

OBSERVE

Now let's look at some verses in which Paul, writing to believers in the city of Colossae, laid out life principles that will help us as we seek to live in our forgiveness.

Leader: Read Colossians 3:1–10 aloud. Have the group say aloud and...
- *circle every occurrence of the words **you** and **your**.*
- *underline **Paul's instructions** to the believers.*

DISCUSS

• What did you learn from marking *you* and *your* in this passage?

• What are believers instructed to do in this passage?

• Discuss how this plays out in practical terms with respect to forgiveness.

• What is Paul's instruction to believers in verse 5?

• How will our obedience to this instruction be evident in our lives?

• The word *but* in verse 8 points to a contrast. What is being contrasted?

• What is the believer to put aside? Why?

greed, which amounts to idolatry.

6 For it is because of these things that the wrath of God will come upon the sons of disobedience,

7 and in them you also once walked, when you were living in them.

8 But now you also, put them all aside: anger, wrath, malice, slander, and abusive speech from your mouth.

9 Do not lie to one another, since you laid aside the old self with its evil practices,

10 and have put on the new self who is being renewed to a true knowledge according to the image of the One who created him.

COLOSSIANS 3:12–15

12 So, as those who have been chosen of God, holy and beloved, put on a heart of compassion, kindness, humility, gentleness and patience;

13 bearing with one another, and forgiving each other, whoever has a complaint against anyone; just as the Lord forgave you, so also should you.

14 Beyond all these things put on love, which is the perfect bond of unity.

15 Let the peace of Christ rule in your hearts, to which indeed you were called in one body; and be thankful.

OBSERVE

Because we're set apart from the world, we belong completely to God. We're "holy," as Paul wrote in the verses we'll look at next. As you read Colossians 3:12–15, watch to see how this impacts our response to those who have hurt us.

Leader: *Read Colossians 3:12–15 aloud. Have the group…*

• *mark the phrase* **put on** *with an arrow:*
↑

• *mark the words* **forgiving** *and* **forgave** *with an* **X.**

INSIGHT

The phrase *put on* means "to envelope yourself, to wrap around, to put on something, like clothing." The idea is to become so immersed in Christ, so focused on Him, that you resemble Him in your thoughts and actions. The verb tense in the Greek indicates this is a command, to be obeyed at once.

DISCUSS

• What is the person chosen of God to "put on" according to verse 12?

• What does verse 13 say is the result of putting on these things?

• What did you learn from marking *forgiving* and *forgave*? By what standard do we measure our forgiveness of others?

• Based on what you read in the Insight Box and what you saw in marking *forgiving* and *forgave,* discuss what you've learned about forgiving those who hurt you. To quote a popular phrase, "What would Jesus do?"

• What does the phrase "whoever has a complaint against anyone" mean?

• What are some typical complaints people have against one another?

EPHESIANS 4:30–32

30 Do not grieve the Holy Spirit of God, by whom you were sealed for the day of redemption.

31 Let all bitterness and wrath and anger and clamor and slander be put away from you, along with all malice.

32 Be kind to one another, tender-hearted, forgiving each other, just as God in Christ also has forgiven you.

OBSERVE

Let's see what else we can learn about how we're to respond to those who have sinned against us.

Leader: Read aloud Ephesians 4:30–32. Have the group...

- *draw a mark like this* ⟿ *over the phrase* **put away.**
- *mark the words* **forgiving** *and* **forgiven** *with an* **X.**

DISCUSS

- According to this passage, what grieves the Holy Spirit?

- What are we to "put away" from ourselves?

INSIGHT

Bitterness refers to a deep-rooted enmity that poisons the inner man. This occurs when we foster hostility toward someone who has hurt us, unintentionally or intentionally. This verse suggests a progression: bitterness leads to wrath (an outward explosion of inner feelings), wrath leads to clamor (a loud outcry against something), and clamor leads to slander (speaking evil about someone).

• Besides grieving the Holy Spirit, what impact can bitterness have on us spiritually, emotionally, and physically and, in turn, on our relationships?

• Do you know of situations where unchecked bitterness wreaked havoc in families, churches, or communities?

Leader: Invite someone to share an example with the group.

1 PETER 2:21-23

21 For you have been called for this purpose, since Christ also suffered for you, leaving you an example for you to follow in His steps,

22 who committed no sin, nor was any deceit found in His mouth;

23 and while being reviled, He did not revile in return; while suffering, He uttered no threats, but kept entrusting Himself to Him who judges righteously.

OBSERVE

Our flesh quickly rejects the idea of offering unconditional forgiveness. After all, if we don't make our enemies pay, who will? It's easy to rationalize and mount a counterattack on those who have hurt us. But what was Jesus' example?

Leader: Read 1 Peter 2:21–23.

• *Have the group mark with a cross* †
every occurrence of **He**, **Himself**, *and* **Him**,
all of which refer to Jesus.

DISCUSS

• What did you learn about Jesus from these verses?

• How can Jesus' example of suffering unjustly at the hands of others help us?

• From all we have seen, is our responsibility to others supposed to be conditional on how they treat us? Explain your answer.

WRAP IT UP

God not only tells us in His Word what we need to do, He gives us an incredible example to follow in the life and death of His Son. Jesus set the standard for forgiveness in His refusal to "make them pay," His silent acceptance of wrongs against Him, and His prayer for forgiveness. The magnitude of this is all the more clear when we realize that our personal sin played an active role in putting Jesus on the cross. We bear responsibility for His death—as if we drove the nails into His hands and feet ourselves.

The forgiveness Jesus offered us through His death on the cross is the same forgiveness we must extend to others. What about you? Are you willing to follow His example?

It's crucial that you forgive those who treat you unjustly, whether or not they repent and regardless of how you feel. It's easy to respond wrongly when you live by your feelings. If you choose, however, to obey God's Word, your feelings eventually catch up to what your mind knows is right.

But how does one forgive when there is no desire to?

First, you must realize that forgiveness is a choice, not an emotion. Since God commanded us to forgive others, to *not* do so is to refuse to obey God. This is not a suggestion but a command to be obeyed regardless of our thoughts or feelings.

Second, you need to know your forgiveness of others does not let them off the hook with God. Your forgiveness does not mean they won't be held accountable to the Lord for what they've done.

Jesus bore sin in His body and consequently forgave when He

hung on the cross, but all unrepentant sin will be judged by God (Hebrews 10:26–27; 2 Thessalonians 1:6–9). In other words, if people don't repent and believe in Him, they will go to hell. Forgiveness is offered, but not apart from receiving Jesus Christ as Lord and Savior.

As a believer, you are to manifest the character and love of Jesus Christ by forgiving even those who have physically, emotionally, sexually, or mentally abused you, just as Christ forgave those who trespassed against Him. To refuse to do this is to keep people from seeing the character of Christ. However, if your forgiveness doesn't lead them to repentance, they are all the more without excuse. They have seen with their own eyes and heard with their own ears a demonstration of the reality of the gospel of Christ (Matthew 11:22–24, 12:41–42, and Revelation 20:11–13).

If, even in the face of these truths, you're still struggling to forgive another person, you need to **take a good hard look at the Lord's forgiveness of you.** Remember, when you forgive another person, you're just one sinner forgiving another. Neither of you is what you ought to be. But when God forgives us, He's forgiving someone who has sinned against perfect holiness.

---

* Adapted from *Lord, Heal My Hurts* by Kay Arthur (Colorado Springs, CO: WaterBrook Press, 1989, 2000).

So far in our study we have seen that we need to forgive and extend mercy to others, and we learned how this was possible. We also learned how to respond to those who have hurt us and aren't repentant. Now the question is, *How do I know if I have truly forgiven someone?* This week we are going to find the answer to that question.

OBSERVE

In Jesus' day, when a rabbi came to dinner, it was customary for people to hang around and listen to his teachings.

Leader: Read Luke 7:36–39. Have the group say aloud and...
- *circle every reference to **the woman,** including pronouns.*
- *mark every reference to **the Pharisee,** including pronouns, with a **P.***

DISCUSS

- What did you learn from marking the references to *the woman* in this passage?

LUKE 7:36–39

36 Now one of the Pharisees was requesting Him [Jesus] to dine with him, and He entered the Pharisee's house and reclined at the table.

37 And there was a woman in the city who was a sinner; and when she learned that He was reclining at the table in the Pharisee's house, she brought an alabaster vial of perfume,

38 and standing behind Him at His feet, weeping, she

began to wet His feet with her tears, and kept wiping them with the hair of her head, and kissing His feet and anointing them with the perfume.

39 Now when the Pharisee who had invited Him saw this, he said to himself, "If this man were a prophet He would know who and what sort of person this woman is who is touching Him, that she is a sinner."

• What did the Pharisee think about all this?

INSIGHT

Pharisees were the religious conservatives of the day. They were self-righteous, seeking distinction and praise for outward observances of rites like ceremonial washings, fasting, prayers, and almsgiving. They neglected genuine piety, priding themselves on their good works and emphasizing the outward appearance rather than the internal condition of the heart.

The alabaster vial contained perfume, which at that time was probably quite costly.

OBSERVE

Leader: Read Luke 7:40–48 aloud and have the group…

- *mark every reference to Simon, the Pharisee, with a P. Be sure to watch carefully for pronouns.*
- *circle every reference to the woman, including pronouns.*

Leader: Read Luke 7:40–48 again. This time have the group…

- *mark the words forgave and forgiven with an X.*
- *mark each reference to love with a heart:* ♡

DISCUSS

- Why did Jesus tell the story of the moneylender?

- How does the point of the story relate to Simon? the women? us?

- Discuss how we may see this scenario played out today.

LUKE 7:40–48

40 And Jesus answered him, "Simon, I have something to say to you." And he replied, "Say it, Teacher."

41 "A moneylender had two debtors: one owed five hundred denarii, and the other fifty.

42 "When they were unable to repay, he graciously forgave them both. So which of them will love him more?"

43 Simon answered and said, "I suppose the one whom he forgave more." And He said to him, "You have judged correctly."

44 Turning toward the woman, He said to Simon, "Do you see this woman? I entered your house; you gave Me no water for My feet, but she has wet My feet with her tears and wiped them with her hair.

45 "You gave Me no kiss; but she, since the time I came in, has not ceased to kiss My feet.

46 "You did not anoint My head with oil, but she anointed My feet with perfume.

47 "For this reason I say to you, her sins, which are many, have been forgiven, for she loved much; but he who is forgiven little, loves little."

48 Then He said to her, "Your sins have been forgiven."

• What similarities did you notice between the story in verses 41 and 42 and Jesus' words in verses 47 and 48?

• What did you learn about the woman's sins? Was she aware of them? Explain your answer.

• What did you learn about Simon in regard to his sins? Was he aware of them? Explain your answer.

• The woman was not forgiven because she loved; rather she loved because she was forgiven. What did you learn about how the proportion of love shown relates to the proportion of forgiveness received?

• How does understanding the depth of your sin impact your thoughts and actions when it comes to forgiveness?

• Who are you more like—the woman who realized she was a sinner and waited on Jesus in tears and humility or Simon who was externally righteous? What evidence does your life give to support your answer?

OBSERVE

We have looked at the following passage several times in this study from different perspectives. So far from these verses we have seen that we are to forgive and that it just doesn't happen; we are responsible for making it happen. Now we're going to see the result of true forgiveness and what that will look like in our lives.

Leader: Read Colossians 3:12–15 aloud. Have the group say aloud and...
- *draw an arrow ↑ over each occurrence of the phrase* **put on.**
- *mark the words* **forgiving** *and* **forgave** *with an* **X.**
- *mark each reference to* **heart** *and* **love** *with a heart:* ♡

DISCUSS

- Discuss what you learned from marking the references to forgiveness.

COLOSSIANS 3:12–15

12 So, as those who have been chosen of God [believers], holy and beloved, put on a heart of compassion, kindness, humility, gentleness and patience;

13 bearing with one another, and forgiving each other, whoever has a complaint against anyone; just as the Lord forgave you, so also should you.

14 Beyond all these things put on love, which is the perfect bond of unity.

15 Let the peace of Christ rule in your hearts, to which indeed you were called in one body; and be thankful.

• According to verse 12, if you choose to forgive, what do you "put on" that will help you do this? Explain how it will enable you to forgive.

INSIGHT

Bearing with one another means "to put up with one another." Grudges have no place in the body of Christ. They lead to anger, wrath, malice, slander, abusive speech, and lying—the sins believers have already been instructed to put aside in (Colossians 3:8–9).

• Discuss the impact that bearing with one another would have in the lives of believers, the church, and our communities if we actually practiced it.

• To what extent did the Lord forgive, and how does that relate to us as believers?

INSIGHT

How can you know when you have truly forgiven from the heart? By the peace you will experience.

"Let the peace of Christ rule" is not a command; rather it is an indicator. A lack of peace indicates that God's Word has been disobeyed.

In this verse *rule* is an athletic term that means "to reside at the game and distribute the prizes." The word actually means "umpire." If there are differences among believers, the peace of God will umpire our hearts. When relationships are broken between believers, it is because one or both are out of fellowship with God.

• According to verse 14, what else are we to "put on" and how is it described? How does it come into play in interpersonal relationships? Explain your answer.

• From what you have seen in the Insight Box as well as what you read in verse 15, what would be a good indicator that you have truly forgiven from your heart?

• Describe what this would look like in the life of a believer based on all we've seen so far in this study.

1 JOHN 4:19

¹⁹ We love, because He first loved us.

EPHESIANS 4:31–5:2

³¹ Let all bitterness and wrath and anger and clamor and slander be put away from you, along with all malice.

³² Be kind to one another, tender-hearted, forgiving each other, just as God in Christ also has forgiven you.

OBSERVE

Leader: Read 1 John 4:19 and Ephesians 4:31–5:2 aloud. Have the group say aloud and mark…

• *the words **forgiving** and **forgiven** with an* **X.**

• *each occurrence of **beloved, love,** and **loved** with a heart.* ♡

DISCUSS

• What did you learn from marking the references to love?

• What did you learn from marking the references to forgiveness?

• Discuss how the things in verse 31 become apparent when we don't forgive— when we're full of bitterness because we've been hurt.

5:1 Therefore be imitators of God, as beloved children;

2 and walk in love, just as Christ also loved you and gave Himself up for us, an offering and a sacrifice to God as a fragrant aroma.

OBSERVE

One of the members of the Corinthian church had caused Paul a great deal of pain, and in response the apostle revealed a compassionate heart. Note the evidence of Paul's love and the example he set as he wrote to the church, urging the believers to forgive the man who'd wounded him.

Leader: Read 2 Corinthians 2:5–11 aloud. Have the group say and mark:
- *each occurrence of **forgive** and **forgiven** with an X.*
- *the word **love** with a heart.*

2 CORINTHIANS 2:5–11

5 But if any has caused sorrow, he has caused sorrow not to me, but in some degree—in order not to say too much—to all of you.

6 Sufficient for such a one is this punishment which was inflicted by the majority,

7 so that on the contrary you should rather forgive and comfort him, otherwise such a one might be overwhelmed by excessive sorrow.

8 Wherefore I urge you to reaffirm your love for him.

9 For to this end also I wrote, so that I might put you to the test, whether you are obedient in all things.

10 But one whom you forgive anything, I forgive also; for indeed what I have forgiven, if I have forgiven anything, I did it for your sakes in the presence of Christ,

DISCUSS

• What did you learn from marking the references to forgiveness in this passage?

• In a sense, forgiveness is the medicine that helps to heal broken hearts. Why is it to be administered, according to verse 7?

• Describe a time when someone you know sinned and forgiveness was extended. What difference did it make?

• Why did Paul urge the Corinthians to reaffirm their love for the man who had wounded him? What would their doing so accomplish?

• According to verse 11, what can happen when we refuse to forgive and love?

• Can you see that the more you compre-
hend the greatness of God's forgiveness of
you, the more you will love? And the
more you love, the easier it will be to forgive? Remember, forgiveness is a matter
of your will—the choice to obey God
regardless of your emotions. As you
choose to walk according to God's Word,
you will soon see your emotions come
into line as well.

[11] so that no advan-
tage would be taken
of us by Satan, for we
are not ignorant of his
schemes.

*Leader: If time allows, use the next few
moments to have the group go before the Lord
and ask His forgiveness for loving others
imperfectly and for holding unforgiving attitudes toward those who have wronged them.
If you don't have enough time for this now,
encourage them to spend time in prayer on
their own later.*

WRAP IT UP

True forgiveness of others will create a love that replaces hatred. When we speak of love, we aren't talking about "warm fuzzy feelings" but about action. *Love* is an action verb. As "imitators of God," you are to "walk in love, just as Christ also loved you, and gave Himself up for us, an offering and a sacrifice to God as a fragrant aroma" (Ephesians 5:1–2).

Loving someone you've forgiven may be hard, but true forgiveness will make the sacrifice. Forgiveness and love are like conjoined twins sharing a single heart. Jesus didn't forgive you, then refuse to love you or have anything to do with you! On the contrary, Jesus *longs* to have fellowship with you. He forgives you and treats you as if you have never sinned against Him. That is God's type of forgiveness, and your forgiveness is to be like His. Accordingly, if you say you've forgiven someone but don't want anything to do with him, you need to go back to God and ask what is keeping you from loving this person. "If someone says, 'I love God,' and hates his brother, he is a liar; for the one who does not love his brother whom he has seen, cannot love God whom he has not seen. And this commandment we have from Him, that the one who loves God should love his brother also" (1 John 4:20–21).

As we bring this week's study to a close, let's look at a father's letter to his adult son.

Dear Son,

I've spent most of my life looking back lamenting the disappointment I caused my parents while continuing to make bad decisions for my life, when the real fire I should have been fighting was being neglected. I am not trying to escape responsibility when I say this, but even though I knew right from wrong, I was incredibly immature and naive to the point of being incompetent.

You have always shown respect for me, always, and I deserved very little. With all the accomplishments you have received in your lifetime you could write a book. You have always been willing to share these accomplishments with me as though I was somehow instrumental in your success, and I would gladly accept that role. However, we both know I contributed very little. In fact, you did these things in spite of me, not because of me. I never received the condemnation I deserved from my mom years ago, and I never got it from you either.

I recently looked at a bunch of old pictures. Several were of you, and I discovered something I had never noticed before. The older ones were of a carefree kid standing by the mailbox or standing in front of the old barn—without a care in the world. The later ones reflected something different: your eyes began to show anger and bitterness. Subtle but irrepressible, the sweetness was drying up like a desert mirage, but it never totally left you. You, as a young man that Satan so desperately wanted, could never outrun the shadow of the cross, indelibly stamped across your life by the relentless prayers of a grandmother you barely remember.

Son, I ask to be relieved of this burden of debt by asking for forgiveness, which I've already received but never quite got around to asking you for. One last thing, there never was a time and never will be that I didn't love you.

Dad

The son had forgiven the father years before. That forgiveness enabled him to show respect and love toward his father. That love and respect contributed to the father being able to write to ask his son for forgiveness. Unlike the family scenario we saw at the beginning of our study, this family experienced the power of forgiveness unleashed in their lives—their hearts were healed, their relationships restored, and their bonds renewed and strengthened.

Only the power of forgiveness unleashed can bring about this kind of restoration and healing. What about you? Are you willing to say, "God, out of uncompromising obedience to You, I want to forgive. Help me!"?

Is it possible to overcome the past? If so, how? Although we cannot change what's happened in our lives, we can change its effect on us by choosing forgiveness.

As we bring this study to a close, let's learn what final steps we need to take in order to unleash the power of forgiveness in our lives.

OBSERVE

If you find yourself wrestling with the concept of forgiveness, especially in light of the pain you've endured, two questions must be answered. Let's consider the first one: "Do you really want to get well?" That seems like a strange question doesn't it? But your answer points to a vital truth.

Leader: *Read aloud John 5:1–9. Have the group say aloud and…*

* *mark each reference to **Jesus,** including the pronouns and synonyms, with a cross:* †
* *underline each reference to **the sick man,** including pronouns.*

JOHN 5:1–9

¹ After these things there was a feast of the Jews, and Jesus went up to Jerusalem.

² Now there is in Jerusalem by the sheep gate a pool, which is called in Hebrew Bethesda, having five porticoes.

³ In these lay a multitude of those who were sick, blind, lame, and withered, [waiting for the moving of the waters;

⁴ for an angel of the Lord went down at certain seasons into the pool and stirred up the water; whoever then first, after the stirring up of the water, stepped in was made well from whatever disease with which he was afflicted.]

⁵ A man was there who had been ill for thirty-eight years.

⁶ When Jesus saw him lying there, and knew that he had already been a long time in that condition, He said to him, "Do you wish to get well?"

⁷ The sick man answered Him, "Sir, I have no man to put me into the pool when the water is stirred up, but

DISCUSS

• What did you learn from marking the references to the sick man Jesus encountered in this passage?

• Jesus asked the sick man a seemingly strange question, given how long he'd been sick. What was the question, and why do you think Jesus asked it?

• How did the man reply? Did he answer Jesus' question? Explain your answer.

• What about you? How would you respond if Jesus were to ask you this question? Don't answer out loud, just think about it.

• Since we've broached the subject of whether or not you really want to get well, it may be helpful to write out your hesitations, fears, and questions related to healing the wounds of your past. Later you can go back and see how God has dealt with them.

Leader: *Allow time for your group to reflect on this.*

while I am coming, another steps down before me."

⁸ Jesus said to him, "Get up, pick up your pallet and walk."

⁹ Immediately the man became well, and picked up his pallet and began to walk. Now it was the Sabbath on that day.

OBSERVE

If you've said yes in answer to the question of whether you really want to get well, the next question is, Are you willing to do what it takes to get better on God's terms? In other words, are you willing to forgive, or are you determined to try to find healing in your own way and on your own terms?

We've already looked at Ephesians 4:31–32 several times; however, let's consider this powerful passage once more in light of the questions we're asking.

EPHESIANS 4:31–32

31 Let all bitterness and wrath and anger and clamor and slander be put away from you, along with all malice.

32 Be kind to one another, tender-hearted, forgiving each other, just as God in Christ also has forgiven you.

HEBREWS 12:15

15 See to it that no one comes short of the grace of God; that no root of bitterness springing up causes trouble, and by it many be defiled.

Leader: Read Ephesians 4:31–32 and Hebrews 12:15 aloud.

- *Have the group draw a squiggly line under **bitterness** and **root of bitterness**, like this:* ∿∿∿∿

DISCUSS

- What did you learn from marking the references to bitterness?

- From these passages what did you learn about the believer's responsibility when it comes to bitterness?

- What is the believer to "put away" according to Ephesians 4:31?

- Having put away these things, what is the believer then supposed to do?

- What is the relationship between the characteristics described in verse 31 and verse 32?

OBSERVE

Leader: Read Psalm 139:23–24. Have the group say aloud and...

- *underline each occurrence of the pronouns **me** and **my**.*
- *mark every reference to **God** with a triangle:* △

DISCUSS

• Who was the psalmist addressing?

• Based on what you observed from marking the pronouns *me* and *my,* what is it the psalmist is asking? List each request.

• Did the psalmist believe God is capable of doing this?

• May we suggest that you take some time to get alone with Lord and ask God to do

23 Search me, O God, and know my heart; try me and know my anxious thoughts;

24 and see if there be any hurtful way in me, and lead me in the everlasting way.

the same for you? If you have buried something, and it needs to be dealt with, God can bring it to light. The hardest part is deciding to ask Him.

We are not saying you need to uncover things the Lord has blotted out. However, as believers we should be open to allowing God to expose any unforgiveness in our lives so that the healing balm of Gilead can be applied. When God reveals those anxious thoughts and hurtful ways, He does so in order to help you in your healing process. If and when God reveals things, don't discount them or assume you have already dealt with them. He is showing them to you because you may have simply denied them or covered them over, and they have been in there festering. Know this: He is the omniscient One, the One who knows you better than you know yourself. These things must be dealt with in order to begin your healing process. Remember, He is a God who loves you and seeks your highest good.

Are you willing to pray and ask God to do this? (This doesn't need to be answered out loud.)

OBSERVE

Leader: Read Philippians 3:13–14 and Isaiah 43:18–19, 25. Have the group say aloud and…

- *draw a mark like this* ⟿ *over the phrases* **what lies behind, former things,** *and* **things of the past.**
- *draw a cloud like this* ☁ *over the words* **forgetting, do not call to mind,** *and* **ponder.**

DISCUSS

- According to these passages, what are believers to do with regard to the past?

INSIGHT

By forgetting, not calling to mind, or not pondering something, we simply choose to no longer be influenced or affected by it. God does not ask us to perform some impossible feat of mental and psychological gymnastics to erase the hurts of the past. We cannot change what lies behind us. However, forgiveness changes the effect the past will have on our future.

PHILIPPIANS 3:13–14

13 Brethren, I do not regard myself as having laid hold of it yet; but one thing I do: forgetting what lies behind and reaching forward to what lies ahead,

14 I press on toward the goal for the prize of the upward call of God in Christ Jesus.

ISAIAH 43:18–19, 25

18 "Do not call to mind the former things, or ponder things of the past.

19 "Behold, I will do something new, now it will spring forth; will you not be aware of it? I will even make a roadway in the wilderness, rivers in the desert.

25 "I, even I, am the one who wipes out your transgressions for My own sake, and I will not remember your sins."

• According to Philippians 3:13–14, what else has Paul determined to do in which we can follow his example?

INSIGHT

The phrase *I press* carries the idea of intense endeavor. The Greeks used this wording to describe a hunter eagerly pursuing his prey. A man does not become a winning athlete by listening to lectures, watching movies, reading books, or cheering at the games. He becomes a winning athlete by getting into the game and determining to win. In the same way, you are to press on, determined to overcome your past.

• Discuss how understanding these truths might affect your life. What are some practical steps you can take when memories of past hurts plague your mind?

OBSERVE

Last week we looked at 2 Corinthians 2 from Paul's perspective, studying his example of compassion for a man who had caused him great pain. Let's look again at this same passage, this time considering the perspective of the church and how unforgiveness will affect it.

Many scholars believe 2 Corinthians 2 is connected to 1 Corinthians 5:1, where Paul admonished the church at Corinth to punish a man who'd been openly living in sin. The church apparently had followed his instructions, resulting in the offender's repentance. The church, however, seems to have refused to welcome the man back.

Leader: Have the group read 2 Corinthians 2:5–11 and…

- *underline each reference to **the offender**, when indicated by the pronouns **he** and **him**.*
- *circle each occurrence of **you** and **your**.*
- *mark each occurrence of **forgive** and **forgiven** with an **X**.*

2 CORINTHIANS 2:5–11

5 But if any has caused sorrow, he has caused sorrow not to me, but in some degree—in order not to say too much—to all of you.

6 Sufficient for such a one is this punishment which was inflicted by the majority,

7 so that on the contrary you should rather forgive and comfort him, otherwise such a one might be overwhelmed by excessive sorrow.

8 Wherefore I urge you to reaffirm your love for him.

9 For to this end also I wrote, so that I might put you to the test, whether you are obedient in all things.

10 But one whom you forgive anything, I forgive also; for indeed what I have forgiven, if I have forgiven anything, I did it for your sakes in the presence of Christ,

11 so that no advantage would be taken of us by Satan, for we are not ignorant of his schemes.

DISCUSS

• What did you learn from marking the references to the offender?

• For whom, besides Paul, had the offender caused trouble?

• What did Paul instruct the church at Corinth to do in regard to the offender?

• From what we have seen, did Paul demand a public or a personal apology?

• What does this passage indicate about Paul's attitude toward the offender?

• From what Paul wrote, what attitude did the church seem to have toward the offender?

• Many of us seem to be easily offended. And when others express outrage at some offense we've endured, we tend to encourage their indignation and play the martyr. Our natural tendency is to feel justified in making the offender suffer and pay. What about you? Are you easily offended? Do you enjoy when others express outrage on your behalf and take up your cause? If you answered yes to these questions, determine today to respond as Paul did so that you will be ready when you next face an opportunity to take offense.

Leader: If time allows, invite someone in the group to describe a situation in which they encouraged others to share in their outrage— along with how they might handle similar situations differently in the future.

• What reason did Paul give in verse 11 for urging the church to forgive?

• Discuss some ways unforgiveness could play a role in Satan's schemes.

• Paul demonstrated the wonderful virtue of true love in action, refusing to take offense or allow others to do so on his behalf: "[Love] does not take into account a wrong suffered" (1 Corinthians 13:4–5). Discuss how it might impact not only the church but also the world if all believers determined to follow his example.

LUKE 23:33–34

33 When they came to the place called The Skull, there they crucified Him and the criminals, one on the right and the other on the left.

34 But Jesus was saying, "Father, forgive them; for they do not know what they are doing." And they cast lots, dividing up His garments among themselves.

ACTS 7:59–60

59 They went on stoning Stephen as he called on the Lord and said, "Lord Jesus, receive my spirit!"

60 Then falling on his knees, he cried out with a loud voice, "Lord, do not hold this sin against them!" Having said this, he fell asleep.

OBSERVE

As we bring this study to a close, let's look at two more examples of those who chose forgiveness rather than bitterness, even in the face of grave injustice.

Leader: Read Luke 23:33–34 and Acts 7:59–60.

- *Have the group mark the words **forgive** and **do not hold this against** with an **X**.*

DISCUSS

- What were the last words of Jesus? the last words of Stephen?

- How does what they suffered compare with the injustice and pain you've endured?

- Discuss what you've learned from Paul, Jesus, and Stephen and how you might apply their examples of forgiveness to your own life.

WRAP IT UP

Do you really want to get well? Are you willing to do what it takes to get better on God's terms? These two questions are not meant to offend. They are asked with your highest good in mind.

Some people love their wounds, their hurts, and their sickness. Why? Some find that their infirmity brings them attention and pity. They glory in parading their afflictions and hurts before others. They may even find a twisted comfort in seeing those who caused their wounds despised by others. How can they exact revenge if their own wounds are healed?

Others cling to their hurts as excuses for what they have become, justification for their shortcomings and failures. They hold the mentality that "I am what I am because of what I suffered. You can't expect anything else!" To be healed would take away their excuses and make them responsible to be what they should be!

Some people are more interested in being angry with God than in experiencing wholeness. They're wrapped up in themselves and don't want to relinquish control. They don't want to risk being obligated to God, to be what He wants them to be.

Others fear change; they simply wouldn't know how to live if they were healed. In a sense, they've become "comfortable" in their pain. They know how to live with it and what to expect. They fear the unknown, having to learn new ways of living.

Many simply are so angry, so bitter, so wretched, so demoralized, and so numb that healing seems utterly impossible, unthinkable.

But there is hope! No one who desires to be free need remain shackled forever to chains of bitterness and anger. Do you really want to get well? Are you willing to do what it takes to get better on God's terms? If your answer is yes, then the Lord stands ready to "bring good news to the afflicted;…to bind up the brokenhearted,…to proclaim liberty to the captives and freedom to prisoners" (Isaiah 61:1).

Take this week to get before the Lord one on one and take the steps necessary to begin your healing process. It may be difficult at first, but the results will be life changing! By unleashing the power of forgiveness in your life and being made whole, you will be able to effectively carry out the plans and purpose He has for you.

This unique Bible study series from Kay Arthur and the teaching team of Precept Ministries International tackles the issues with which inquiring minds wrestle—in short, easy-to-grasp lessons ideal for small-group settings. The study courses in the series can be followed in any order.

How Do You Know God's Your Father?

by Kay Arthur, David and BJ Lawson

So many say "I'm a Christian," but how can they really know God's their Father—and that heaven's home? The short book of 1 John was written for that purpose—that you might *know* that you really do have eternal life. This is a powerful, enlightening study that will take you out of the dark and open your understanding to this key biblical truth.

Having a Real Relationship with God

by Kay Arthur

For those who yearn to know God and relate to Him in meaningful ways, Kay Arthur opens the Bible to show the way to salvation. With a straightforward examination of vital Bible passages, this enlightening study focuses on where we stand with God, how our sin keeps us from knowing Him, and how Christ bridged the chasm between humans and their Lord.

Being a Disciple: Counting the Real Cost

by Kay Arthur, Tom and Jane Hart

Jesus calls His followers to be disciples. And discipleship comes with a cost, a commitment. This study takes an inductive look at how the Bible describes a disciple, sets forth the marks of a follower of Christ, and invites students to accept the challenge and then enjoy the blessings of discipleship.

How Do You Walk the Walk You Talk?

by Kay Arthur

This thorough, inductive study of Ephesians 4 and 5 is designed to help students see for themselves what God says about the lifestyle of a true believer in Jesus Christ. The study will equip them to live in a manner worthy of their calling, with the ultimate goal of developing a daily walk with God marked by maturity, Christlikeness, and peace.

Living a Life of True Worship

by Kay Arthur, Bob and Diane Vereen

Worship is one of Christianity's most misunderstood topics. This study explores what the Bible says about worship—what it is, when it happens, where it takes place. Is it based on your emotions? Is it something that only happens on Sunday in church? Does it impact how you serve? This study offers fresh, biblical answers.

Discovering What the Future Holds

by Kay Arthur, Georg Huber

With all that's transpiring in the world, people cannot help but wonder what the future holds. Will there ever be peace on earth? How long will the world live under the threat of terrorism? Is a one-world ruler on the horizon? This easy-to-use study guide leads readers through the book of Daniel, which sets forth God's blueprints for the future.

How to Make Choices You Won't Regret

by Kay Arthur, David and BJ Lawson

Every day we face innumerable decisions, some of which have the potential to change the course of our lives forever. Where do we go for direction? What do we do when faced with temptation? This fast-moving study offers practical, trustworthy guidelines by exploring the role of Scripture and the Holy Spirit in the decision-making process.

Money and Possessions: The Quest for Contentment
by Kay Arthur, David Arthur

Our attitudes toward money and possessions reflect the quality of our relationship with God. And, according to the Scriptures, our view of money reveals where our true affections lie. In this study readers dig into the Scriptures to learn where money comes from, how we're supposed to handle it, and how to live an abundant life, regardless of our financial circumstances.

How Can a Man Control His Thoughts, Desires, and Passions?
by Bob Vereen

This study equips men with the truth that God has provided everything we need to resist temptation. Through the examples of men in Scripture—those who fell into sin and those who stood firm—readers will find hope for controlling their passions, learn how to choose the path of purity, and find assurance that through the power of the Holy Spirit and God's Word, they can stand before God blameless and pure.

Living Victoriously in Difficult Times
by Kay Arthur, Bob and Diane Vereen

We live in a fallen world filled with fallen people, and we cannot escape hardship and pain. Somehow difficult times are a part of God's plan, and they serve His purposes. This study helps readers discover how to glorify God in the midst of their pain. They'll learn how to find joy even when life seems unfair and to experience the peace that comes from trusting in the One whose strength is made perfect in their weaknesses.

Building a Marriage That Really Works
by Kay Arthur, David and BJ Lawson

God designed marriage to be a satisfying, fulfilling relationship, and He created men and women so that they—together and as one flesh—could reflect His love for the world. Marriage, when lived out as God intended, makes us complete, brings us joy, and gives our lives fresh meaning. In this study, readers examine God's design for marriage and learn how to establish and maintain the kind of marriage that brings lasting joy.

Rising to the Call of Leadership
by Kay Arthur, David and BJ Lawson

What does God expect of those He places in positions of authority? What characteristics mark the truly effective leader? And how can you be the leader God has called you to be? You'll find the answers to these questions and more in this study of four important leaders of Israel—Eli, Samuel, Saul, and David—whose lives point to principles we need to know as leaders in our homes, in our communities, in our churches, and ultimately in our world.

The Essentials of Effective Prayer
by Kay Arthur, BJ and David Lawson

This biblical overview of prayer will lead you to a more vibrant prayer life as you learn what God expects from your prayers and what you can expect from Him. A detailed examination of the Lord's Prayer and powerful principles drawn from other examples of prayer throughout the Bible will challenge you to a deeper understanding of God's will, His way, and His love for you as you experience what it truly means to draw near to God in prayer.